W9-CGM-433

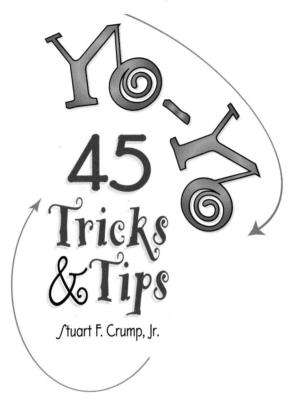

Yo-Yo

45

Tricks & Tips

Stuart F. Crump, Jr.

Publications International, Ltd.

Working with a yo-yo can be a dangerous activity and can result in serious injury. Do not practice yo-yo tricks in a crowded area or near windows. Do not let children under 7 play with yo-yos, and all children should be supervised by adults, as the string could cause choking or other serious injury. The publisher, authors, and consultants specifically disclaim liability for any loss or injury incurred as a consequence of the use and application, either directly or indirectly, of any advice or information presented herein.

The brand-name products mentioned or shown in this publication are servicemarks or trademarks of their respective companies. The mention of any product is merely a record of the procedure used and does not constitute an endorsement by the respective proprietors of Publications International, Ltd., nor does it constitute an endorsement by any of these companies that their products should be used in the manner recommended by this publication.

Contents

Introduction

Yo-yo popularity, much like the toy itself, goes up and down, sometimes sleeping and sometimes flying. Today the yo-yo is more popular than ever. Not only are kids discovering the joys of yo-yoing, but adults, too, are rediscovering what they loved about the yo-yo when they were young.

Yo-Yo History

No one really knows who first put two disks together with a small axle separating the halves and then tied a string to the axle and wound it up. Some historians say it was developed in ancient Greece, India, or China. We do know, however, that the toy first became popular in both England and France in the late 18th century.

The first modern yo-yos were introduced in the United States by Donald F. Duncan in the late 1920s. He is credited with popularizing (though probably not inventing) the slip-string yo-yo, which enables a yo-yo to "sleep."

The yo-yo first became popular in the 1930s, when Duncan sent out teams of traveling yo-yo men (not women, mind you) who would spend three, four, and five weeks in cities and towns across America, teaching tricks, selling yo-yos, and running contests. The yo-yo reached fad levels in the late 1940s, throughout the 1950s, and into the early 1960s. By then almost every kid in America had a yo-yo.

But the Golden Days of Yo-Yo unfortunately ended when Duncan, who had manufactured more yo-yos than it could sell, went bankrupt in 1965, shortly after the yo-yo boom had suddenly ended. The traveling professional yo-yoers soon disappeared, and the toy began to lose some of its appeal.

However, the yo-yo was not to be defeated. It experienced a major revival in the early 1970s, and today, the yo-yo is experiencing its greatest popularity yet. Why is it so popular? Many "baby boomers" who reached the prime of their youth during the Golden Days of Yo-Yo have now reached adulthood and have children of their own. Together both adults and children are rediscovering its charm.

Some of them have even turned that interest into a new career. Tom Smothers is the most famous, with his hit Yo-Yo Man routine of stage and TV fame, which he has been performing since about 1980. Dr. Tom Kuhn, a California dentist who loved the yo-yo as a child, was re-bitten by the yo-yo bug in 1980. He went on a quest (which continues to this day) to find the "perfect" yo-yo. During that time he has introduced an array of delightful high-performance yo-yos such as the Silver Bullet (made from aircraft aluminum), the SB-2 ball-bearing-axle yo-yo, the Roller Woody, and the Sleep Machine. He now spends almost as much time with his yo-yo business as his dentist business.

In the late 1990s, several yo-yo companies once again began sending out teams of traveling yo-yo men and women. The presence of these teams in the field has also helped rekindle the new yo-yo boom, which began in late 1997 and reached fever pitch in 1998 and 1999.

Perhaps more than any other toy, the yo-yo has had its ups and downs. But one thing is certain: The yo-yo keeps coming back!

Selecting Your Yo-Yo

When choosing a yo-yo, it is important to stick to one of the more popular names such as Duncan, Playmaxx, What's Next, Tom Kuhn Custom Yo-Yos, or Yomega. Beware of cheaply made brands. They are much more difficult to play with. Spend a little extra money and get a better yo-yo.

Non-Sleeping Yo-Yo

A non-sleeping yo-yo can only be used to perform about a half-dozen tricks. It is perfect for beginners. When winding up a non-sleeping yo-yo, put the string on your finger and throw the yo-yo down toward the floor. The yo-yo will unwind as it descends. When it reaches the end of the string, kinetic energy will keep the yo-yo spinning. Give the string a tug and the yo-yo will wind back up and return to your hand. (This is similar to the Gravity Pull on page 14.)

Slip-String Yo-Yos

The slip-string yo-yo makes performing a Sleeper possible, which in turn opens up a universe of hundreds of tricks. With a slip-string yo-yo, the string is actually twice as long as it appears to be. It starts at the finger loop, goes all the way down to the yo-yo, wraps around the axle, and continues on back to the finger. The yo-yo sits in a small string loop around the axle. It is this loop that permits the yo-yo to "sleep" until it either stops spinning or is recalled to the hand with a firm jerk.

Ball-bearing and Transaxle Yo-Yos

Transaxle yo-yos are designed to spin for an incredibly long time. With a regular yo-yo, the string loops around the axle. With a transaxle yo-yo, a special, extremely low-resis-tance plastic ring touches the axle. The string wraps around the outside of the ring, but never touches the axle. This allows for extremely long spins and it also gives the string an extremely long life.

In the late 1980s, Tom Kuhn introduced an improved transaxle, the SB-2, which used a ball-bearing ring around the axle. Spins of 30 to 60 seconds or more are common with ball-bearing yo-yos. By comparison, a standard wood-en-axle yo-yo can be made to sleep only about 10-15 sec-onds.

Another invention is the Yo-Yo with a Brain, first intro-duced by Yomega in 1984. The "Brain" Yomega is a plastic yo-yo with a clutch, invented by Mike Caffrey, who would eventually go to work as head of marketing and sales for Duncan.

When the Yomega yo-yo is spinning at full speed, the clutch separates and allows the yo-yo to spin. As the yo-yo slows down, an arrangement of springs inside the yo-yo pushes the clutch halves back together and causes the yo-yo to return to your hand.

The clutch makes it easier for new yo-yoers to learn how to make a yo-yo "sleep."

Basics of Yo

Before you begin, you must first learn the basic funda-mentals of yo-yoing. Keep in mind that most of the modern yo-yos can be taken apart by the user. This feature will come in handy in case your string tangles inside your yo-

yo. To untangle your string, simply unscrew the yo-yo, take the halves apart, detangle the string, put the yo-yo back together, and away you yo.

Making a Yo-Yo Slip Knot

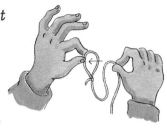

When you take your yo-yo out of the package, you'll notice that the yo-yo comes with a loop tied in one end. Resist your instinct and do not immediately slip that loop over your finger!

Instead, slip the string through that loop and make a slip knot. This is what you will place around your middle finger.

Cutting the String to the Proper Length

If you are more than 5'8", you may be able to use the string at the length it comes out of the package. However, if you are shorter than about 5'8", you'll need to shorten the string. Here's how:

Drop the yo-yo to the floor. Put your forefinger on your belly button. Wrap the top of the string around your forefinger and tie a knot in the string, making a

9

new loop. Carefully cut off the excess string and throw it away.

There is no "correct" string length. Some players prefer a slightly shorter string; others prefer it slightly longer. Experiment to find your ideal length. The belly button length offers a good guideline to get you started.

String Tension, or Tightness

A new yo-yo string will need to be tightened to function properly. Begin by slipping the loop you made over your middle finger. Let the yo-yo drop and rest at the end of the string. If the string is too tight, the yo-yo will spin counterclockwise. If the string is too loose, it will spin clockwise.

A quick way to tighten the string back to the proper state of twist is to take the string off your finger, hold the yo-yo in your hand and let the string dangle down freely. The twist in the string will quickly disappear.

Putting the String on Your Yo-Yo

After constant use, your yo-yo string will become frayed and worn. Try to change the string before it breaks. A string that gives way without warning can launch a dangerous missile and send it flying across the room, generally in a direct line with the head of the person least likely to appreciate your new yo-yo skills.

To remove an old string, first let the yo-yo hang freely. Then grab the string about three inches above the yo-yo. With your other hand, spin the yo-yo in a counterclockwise direction until the two halves of the string start to separate. Then stick your fingers in between the two halves of the string, spread the string apart, and pull the yo-yo free of the string.

To put on a new string, separate the two strands of the string at the unknotted end to create a loop. Slide the yo-yo into this loop in the string. Then twist the string by crossing the strands, allowing the string to twist around the axle of the yo-yo.

Make sure there are no kinks in the string. Most strings are generally too loose and need to be tightened before use. Let the yo-yo hang freely, then spin it clockwise to tighten the string. (See above illustration.)

General Tips

Winding up the Yo-Yo

To wind up a sleeping yo-yo, grab one of the yo-yo disks with the fingers of your free hand. Place your thumb or forefinger over the groove that separates the two halves of the yo-yo and wind the string once over your finger. Lift your finger and wind the string 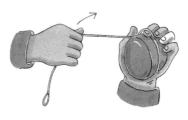 inside the finger for the second and third times around.

For the fourth and subsequent winds, pull your finger out of the loop and wind the loop into the yo-yo. Wind the string lightly until the last couple of loops, which should be wound slightly tighter. Finally, throw your yo-yo down and bring it back up once to clear your string. Now your yo-yo is ready for play.

Challenge Levels

Each trick in this book has been rated with a challenge level: easy, medium, or challenging. Yo-yo symbols above the title of each trick represent the degree of difficulty:

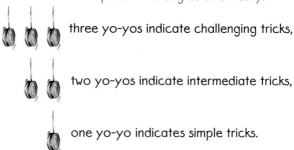

three yo-yos indicate challenging tricks,

two yo-yos indicate intermediate tricks,

one yo-yo indicates simple tricks.

Also, the instructions in this book are written for the right-handed yo-yoer. Don't worry, though. If you are a left-hand-ed, simply reverse the directions when necessary.

Yo-Yo Safety

Some of the tricks in this book, such as Around the World, are potentially dangerous tricks to you, to others, and to your surroundings. When playing with your yo-yo, be sure you have a high ceiling so the yo-yo won't hit it. Also make sure that nothing is in the path of your yo-yo.

Observe the "Circle of Danger" concept. Mentally check out the area around you to make sure there is not a person or an object nearby (within about six feet) that can be potentially hit as you perform your tricks.

The most important tip of all is enjoy your yo-yo and play with it safely!

The Gravity Pull

This is the classic, up-and-down yo-yo trick, the one most people think of when they hear the word "yo-yo."

1. Hold the yo-yo in your yo-yo hand in front of you, palm down, slightly above your waist. Open your hand and let the yo-yo unroll toward the ground.

2. At the precise moment that the yo-yo reaches the end of its unwinding, near the floor, give a firm upward jerk with your hand and the yo-yo will wind up and return to your hand. Presto! You've completed the first step to becoming a yo-yo expert!

Yo-Yo Tip: Do not use your free hand to assist you in catching the yo-yo. Catch it with the same hand that drops it.

The Throw Down

Many yo-yo tricks begin with this simple maneuver or a variation of it. If you do not get it right the first few times, don't panic. All it takes is a bit of practice.

1. Hold your hand out in front of you, palm up. Stand the yo-yo on its edge, placing it between your thumb and middle finger, in line with your shoulder. The string should curl up over the top of the yo-yo, ready to flow out in front of you.

2. With a flick of the wrist, whip the yo-yo to the ground in a firm, overhand motion. Be sure to throw the yo-yo straight down. Don't let it lean to one side or the other. When the yo-yo reaches the end of the string, give a slight tug on the string, and the yo-yo will return home.

The Sleeper

Now that you've learned the Throw Down and the Gravity Pull, you're ready to learn the most important trick of all—the Sleeper. This trick is basically a delayed version of the up-and-down Gravity Pull. More than 90 percent of all yo-yo tricks incorporate the Sleeper in some form. From here, the amount of tricks you can learn is endless!

Yo-Yo Tip: If the yo-yo spins aimlessly at the bottom of the string and refuses to come up, this means the string is too loose. To tighten, let the yo-yo dangle at the end of the string then spin the yo-yo clockwise. If, on the other hand, it snaps immediately back to your hand and refuses to spin, it is wound too tightly. Loosen it by twisting the yo-yo in a counterclockwise direction.

1. The initial motion is precisely the same as what is used in the Throw Down. Hold your yo-yo hand out in front of you with the palm facing up. Remember, the string should come off toward the top and front of the yo-yo.

16

2. With a whipping motion, similar to that used when throwing a fastball, grab the yo-yo and flick it sharply toward the ground. It should stay down—spinning—at the end of the string.

3. While the yo-yo is spinning, turn your yo-yo hand over, palm facing down. If the string tension is correct, the yo-yo should spin at the end of the string for a few seconds. Then give the string a jerk and the yo-yo should quickly return to your hand.

Ancient Grecian urns (c.500 B.C.) on display in museums in Greece show Greek youths playing with yo-yos made out of terra cotta.

The Forward Pass

Although your fans may not jump up and down and cheer as if they were at a football game, they'll applaud when you throw a Forward Pass.

1. Hold the yo-yo as if you were about to perform a Throw Down. But instead of holding your yo-yo hand in front of you, drop it to your side, turning it over so the back of your hand faces forward.

Yo-Yo Tip:
Don't worry if you don't catch it the first few times. If it hits your hand as it returns, you're doing it correctly. With a little practice, you'll learn to catch it every time.

2. Then flick or swing your wrist and arm forward, throwing the yo-yo directly in front of you.

3. When the yo-yo reaches the end of the string, give it a slight tug. Then turn your hand over, palm facing up, and catch the yo-yo in your palm.

Walk the Dog

This dog won't hunt or need a license, but it will perform plenty of tricks. At the end of the trick, give a whistle and "call" your doggie home.

1. To take your "doggie" for a walk, start by throwing a fast Sleeper.

Yo-Yo Tip:
Be careful not to perform this trick on concrete surfaces, such as a sidewalk or a driveway. The rough surface can seriously damage the edge of your yo-yo. The best surface for this trick is a firm rug or carpet.

2. Swing the yo-yo slightly forward and set it lightly on the ground. Let its spinning motion gently pull it along the ground. The yo-yo may snap back to your hand, but keep trying.

3. Before the yo-yo stops spinning, give a slight tug, and the "doggie" will return to your hand.

The Creeper

The Creeper is a variation of Walk the Dog. Another name for this trick is the Land Rover.

1. Begin by throwing a Sleeper while standing in one place. Now, "walk the dog" out to the end of its string.

Yo-Yo Tip:
As with Walk the Dog, be careful not to perform this trick on concrete surfaces, such as a sidewalk or a driveway. The rough surface can seriously damage the edge of your yo-yo. The best surface for this trick is a firm rug or carpet.

2. While the "dog is walking," get down on one knee and give the yo-yo a jerk. It will walk along the floor back to your hand. Creepy!

Sleeping Beauty

Technically speaking, the Sleeping Beauty is not a trick. It is more of a maneuver designed to tighten or loosen the string. It is also known as the Flying Saucer. When this trick is performed properly, it resembles an outer space craft.

Yo-Yo Tip:
Throw the yo-yo to the right side of your body to tighten the string. Throw it to the left side to loosen the string.

1. If you are right-handed, the tightening move is the easier of the two. Hold the yo-yo horizontally in your hand and throw it out to the side. To do this you'll need to throw it slightly on an angle. The yo-yo will then spin on its side with the string loosely revolving around it in the air.

2. While the yo-yo is spinning on its side, reach out and grab the yo-yo string with your left hand about five or six inches above the yo-yo.

3. Pull it up and out from your right side to your left, so the yo-yo looks like a flying saucer. Hold the yo-yo slightly above the height of your right hand. Let it spin on its side for a few seconds.

4. As the yo-yo slows down, give it a little jerk, upward with your left hand and sideways with your right hand, and let the string wind up. The yo-yo will return to your hand.

The first time the term "flying saucer" was used in print occurred in 1947, when pilot Kenneth Arnold, flying a small plane, observed an unidentified flying object shaped like a saucer skipping across the sky. It wouldn't take long before "flying saucer" became part of the English vocabulary.

Around the World

Once you've learned the Sleeper and the Forward Pass, you're ready to take a quick trip Around the World!

1. Start by throwing a Forward Pass.

2. Instead of jerking the yo-yo when it reaches the end of the string, swing it around over your shoulder and behind your back in a full 360-degree arc. The yo-yo should remain at the end of the string throughout the whole trick, spinning as it goes around.

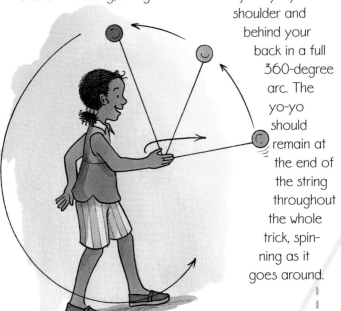

3. When it gets back to the starting point in front of you, jerk the string and bring the yo-yo home.

No one really knows who first put two disks together with a small axle separating them and then tied a string to the axle and wound it up. It may have been a caveman looking for something to do in the evening while waiting for television to be invented.

Around the Corner

If you can travel Around the World, you're ready for a shorter trip that's just Around the Corner! This trick is also known as Orbit Launch.

Yo-Yo Tip: Be sure the yo-yo is spinning swiftly when you tug the string to call it home.

1. Begin by throwing a hard Sleeper.

2. Swing the string around and behind the upper part of your yo-yo arm, so that the yo-yo hangs behind you, draped over the upper part of your yo-yo arm just above the elbow.

3. Reach down with your yo-yo hand and grab the string just above the spinning yo-yo with your thumb and index finger.

4. Now quickly jerk the yo-yo up. It will jump over the top of your arm as it winds up. Let it continue down toward the floor, then retrieve it as if you were doing a Gravity Pull.

Flambeau Plastics, which had been making yo-yos for Duncan, acquired the rights to the "Duncan" name in 1965 after Duncan went bankrupt. Flambeau continues making Duncan Yo-Yos to this day.

Skin the Cat

Skin the Cat is the first step—a building block—for performing some of the more challenging string tricks. It is also called the Tidal Wave.

1. Start by throwing a fast sleeper in front of you.

2. Place the forefinger of your free hand up under the string and slide it up along the string in front of your yo-yo finger.

Kids today are better yo-yoers than ever in the history of the toy. At the World Championship in 1998, none of the finalists were over 19 years old.

3. Now lift your free hand slightly upward. At the same time gently pull backward on the string with your yo-yo hand.

4. When the yo-yo is about six inches from your free hand, flip it upward and out with your free hand's forefinger while simultaneously jerking the string backward with your yo-yo hand. As the yo-yo comes back to your hand, do not catch it. Instead, go into a Forward Pass and whip the yo-yo back out in front of you. Catch it on the return loop.

Rock the Baby

This entertaining trick is probably the most popular trick of all time. Best of all, it's both easy and fun to perform.

1. Begin by throwing a ∫leeper. Lift your yo-yo hand up until it is slightly above your head.

2. Put your free hand out in front of the yo-yo string, fingers stretched apart and the palm facing your body, between the string and your body. As you do this, catch the string about one-third of the way down with the pinky and the tip of the thumb of your free hand.

3. Then grab the string with your yo-yo hand several inches above the yo-yo.

Yo-Yo Tip:
Practice this trick with a "dead" (i.e. nonspinning) yo-yo until you can perform the movements smoothly and flawlessly. Then try it with the *Sleeper*. You will need to have mastered at least a six-second *Sleeper* before performing this trick.

4. In the same motion, bring your yo-yo hand up above your free hand, forming the triangular-shaped cradle. If you've constructed a cradle correctly, the yo-yo will neatly hang in the middle of the triangle of string you've formed between your two hands. Now "rock the baby" to sleep by swinging the spinning yo-yo back and forth in the "cradle."

5. Give the yo-yo a jerk, let go of the string, and the yo-yo will snap back to your hand.

Most historians and linguists agree that the word "yo-yo" comes from the native Philippine language Tagalog, and that it means "come, come."

Bouncing Betsy

Want a date with Bouncing Betsy? This trick is a simple variation of the Gravity Pull. Be careful not to smash your yo-yo!

Yo-Yo Tip: Don't perform this trick on brick, concrete, blacktop, or hardwood surfaces. Carpet or a firm rug is the best surface for this trick.

1. Start with an outward Throw Down so that the yo-yo strikes the floor about 18 to 24 inches in front of you.

2. Then simply allow it to bounce off the floor and return to your hand.

Three-Leaf Clover

Three-Leaf Clovers are just as lucky as Four-Leaf Clovers. Make a wish before performing this trick.

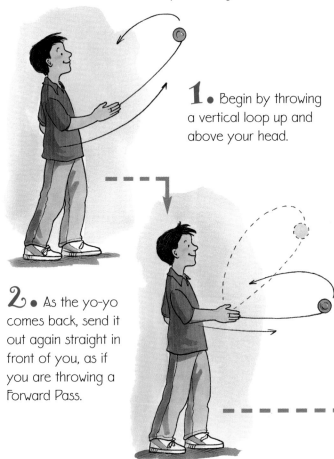

1. Begin by throwing a vertical loop up and above your head.

2. As the yo-yo comes back, send it out again straight in front of you, as if you are throwing a Forward Pass.

3. As it comes back, send it out again, angled down toward the floor as in the Throw Down. Catch it as it comes back up.

To make a Four-Leaf Clover, simply fling the yo-yo straight backward as it returns to your hand from the downward loop.

Over the Falls

Going Over the Falls is not as easy as it looks. But don't let that stop you. The challenge of performing this trick perfectly is worth the wait.

1. Start by throwing a Forward Pass.

2. As it returns to your yo-yo hand, fling it straight down toward the floor. Make a "swishing" sound as your yo-yo goes past your hand and downward. Be sure that the yo-yo passes between your hand and your body.

3. As soon as the yo-yo hits the bottom, give the string a jerk, and it will return to your hand.

Yo-Yo Tip:
Ideally, you should direct the yo-yo straight down, not off at an angle. This will take a bit of practice, but practice makes perfect.

The Breakaway

Like Michael Jordan, you can defy gravity with this trick. When the Breakaway is performed properly, the yo-yo will seem to hang in mid-air for a fraction of a second.

1. Hold the yo-yo in your hand and bend your arm as if you're making a muscle. Swing your arm, release the yo-yo, and bring your elbow down sharply. The yo-yo will fly out and down.

2. If you are a right-handed yo-yoer, swing your arm to the left, across the front of your body in an arc. Let the yo-yo swing out in front of you to the opposite side of your body. Allow the yo-yo to hang in mid-air at the end of the string for a fraction of a second. As the yo-yo slows down, give the string a jerk and call the yo-yo back home.

Texas Cowboy

This trick is similar to Around the World, except that the yo-yo is thrown horizontally instead of vertically.

1. Throw a ∫leeper across your body as if you were about to perform a ∫leeping Beauty (see page 21).

2. Let the yo-yo spin sideways about one foot from the floor and allow it to travel in a circle, as if you were throwing an Around the World horizontally near the floor. As the yo-yo approaches each of your legs, lift one leg at a time and allow the yo-yo to continue its circle.

3. As the yo-yo comes back in front of you, give a jerk on the string and bring the yo-yo back home.

A common myth is that a yo-yo's two halves must be perfectly balanced in shape and weight for a yo-yo to perform well. However, experiments have shown that halves with vastly different weights can be joined together by an axle. The resulting yo-yo will perform well as long as it's spinning. It has something to do with "gyroscopic stability."

Loop the Loop

Loop the Loop is one of the most difficult tricks to learn smoothly. The secret is entirely in the wrist. Don't be discouraged if you don't get it right the first few times. Be persistent, and keep trying! Remember to keep arm movement at a minimum. All the action should be in the wrist.

1. Start with a Forward Pass.

2. As the yo-yo comes back, don't catch it. As it passes your hand on the inside of your arm, snap your wrist forward in a circular motion and send the yo-yo back out again. This will make it loop.

Yo-Yo Tip:
Looping with the right hand will untwist the yo-yo string one-half turn with each loop. Begin your looping with a slightly tightened yo-yo string. Left-handed loops will twist the string tighter by one-half turn with each loop.

3. Do it once. Then try it twice. Then three times. Keep at it. Be sure to keep your arm out in front of you while making loops.

After you've learned how to "loop" with your yo-yo hand, practice "looping" with your other hand. This will be much harder, but the results—however slow they are in coming—will be well worth the effort. Eventually you will want to be able to loop with both hands simultaneously.

41

Outside Loops

Now that you've gone inside with Loop the Loop, it's time to take a trip to the outside with Outside Loops.

1. Begin by throwing a Forward Pass.

2. As the yo-yo returns, let it pass over the top of your yo-yo hand. The palm of your hand should be facing inward. Allow the yo-yo to circle your hand on the outside of the wrist.

Donald F. Duncan helped develop and market other devices in addition to the yo-yo, including the hydraulic automobile brake, the Good Humor truck, and the Eskimo Pie.

3. As it passes your hand on the outside of your arm, swing the yo-yo forward again with another flick of your wrist. Keep your hand low. If you lift it high, it will be hard to catch the yo-yo.

Walk the Tightrope

This daredevil trick is more a maneuver than a trick. It's also a way to wind up your yo-yo.

1. Hold your yo-yo string finger at about eye level and let the yo-yo dangle down around your knees.

2. Take your free hand and loop the string over your forefinger. Bring your yo-yo hand down and grab the yo-yo between the thumb on one side and your ring and pinky fingers on the other side. What you have done is made a loop of string going from the middle finger of your

yo-yo hand around the forefinger of your free hand and back to the yo-yo itself, which is held in the yo-yo hand. Make sure the part of the string that is attached to the middle finger of your yo-yo hand is just below the yo-yo.

3. Let the string hang limply between your hands. Then gently drop the yo-yo onto the string near the right middle finger of your yo-yo hand.

4. Slowly "walk" the yo-yo along the lower string, allowing it to roll up as it goes. Sometimes this maneuver is easier if you hold the string firmly in the free hand, rather than letting it slide over your finger.

5. Once the yo-yo reaches the free hand, grab the yo-yo and finish winding it with the yo-yo hand. If you prefer, you can also drop the yo-yo and wind it up all the way by performing a Gravity Pull (see page 14).

Reverse Sleeper

This maneuver appears to be identical to throwing a regular sleeper. The difference is that in this trick the yo-yo will spin backward when thrown down.

1. Extend your hand out in front of you. Stand the yo-yo on its edge in your yo-yo hand, palm up, as you would when throwing a regular sleeper. Now place the yo-yo between your thumb and middle finger, in line with your shoulder. Unlike the sleeper, the string should flow out of the back and the bottom of the yo-yo.

2. With a flick of the wrist, whip the yo-yo to the ground in a firm, overhand motion. Make sure to throw the yo-yo straight down,

Yo-Yo Tip: This trick is not usually performed for its own sake (because it looks so similar to a regular sleeper) but rather is used as the first step with certain tricks, such as Walk the Cat and the Guillotine.

Research conducted at the University of Karlsruhe in Germany about the science and physics of the yo-yo revealed that the yo-yo reaches its maximum spin speed at the half-way point on its way down the string.

otherwise it may spin out on its side. Watch the yo-yo spin back-ward when thrown down.

3. Give the string a jerk and the yo-yo should quickly return to your hand.

Hop the Fence

This trick is similar to Loop the Loop, except that the yo-yo is directed down toward the floor rather than out in front of you.

1. Start this trick with a Throw Down.

2. As the yo-yo returns to your hand, don't catch it. Instead allow it to "hop" over the top of your hand. Then, with a flick of your wrist, send it back down toward the floor. Keep "hopping." With a little practice, you'll be able to "hop the fence" for as long as you want.

If you're really adventurous, try performing Milk the Cow. Place a yo-yo in each of your hands and Hop the Fence alternately with your right and left hands. This trick may require more time to perfect.

Walk the Cat

Cats never do what you want them to do or go where you want them to go. When performed smoothly, this fun and funny trick will always get a big laugh.

1. Begin by throwing a Reverse Sleeper.

2. While slowly walking forward, touch the yo-yo to the ground. Because the yo-yo is spinning backward, it will "walk" backward behind you.

3. Pretend that you weren't expecting it to go in that direction. As the yo-yo reaches the end of its walking area, let it jerk your whole body backward as if the "cat" has suddenly pulled you off balance.

The Guillotine

Despite its dangerous name, this trick is perfectly safe when performed correctly.

Yo-Yo Tip:
Be sure to throw a Reverse Sleeper. Otherwise the yo-yo may strike your neck or your mouth and not feel particularly pleasant.

1. Begin by throwing a Reverse Sleeper.

2. Lift the yo-yo up with your yo-yo hand, lower your head, and loop the string over your neck.

3. Give the string a slight jerk. The yo-yo will jump up and over your head and return to your hand.

It has been said that French aristocrats played with their yo-yos while on their way to the guillotine during the Reign of Terror in late 18th Century France.

Dog Bite

The key to performing this trick is to not announce it in advance. Pretend that the "bite" occurs without your realizing it. When your yo-yo bites, look puzzled as if your yo-yo has "disappeared." Slowly turn around as if you are looking for it. Your audience will laugh when they see the yo-yo behind you, stuck on the back of your pant leg.

Yo-Yo Tip:

Make sure you wear lightweight, loose fitting pants when performing this trick. You may have to do some experimenting as well. Some fabrics are easier for your yo-yo to grab than others.

1. Begin by throwing a fast Sleeper.

2. Standing with your feet approximately two feet apart, swing the yo-yo between your legs and below the knee.

3. Jerk the string and time the return so that the yo-yo brushes against the underside of your pant leg as it returns. The yo-yo should grab the fabric of your pants and "bite" your leg.

The earliest Duncan demonstrators earned a whopping $15 a week, a very good salary for a young man during the Great Depression.

Buzz Saw

You can do amazing things with a yo-yo, as you know. But did you know you can turn it into a noisy Buzz Saw? Find out how with this fun sound-effect trick.

Yo-Yo Tip:
Make sure you tell the person holding the paper to watch the spinning yo-yo so it doesn't suddenly move forward!

1. Start by throwing a hard sleeper.

2. Then have a friend hold a piece of paper tightly between his or her hands parallel to the ground. Gently touch the spinning yo-yo to the paper. The spinning yo-yo will create a sound like a power saw.

The Motorcycle

This "motorcycle" may not win a lot of races, but it sure is fun to drive.

1. Start by throwing a fast Sleeper.

2. With your free hand, grab the string between your thumb and forefinger, about six inches from your yo-yo hand.

3. Lift the string your free hand is clutching above your yo-yo hand. Grab the string between your yo-yo hand's middle finger and thumb.

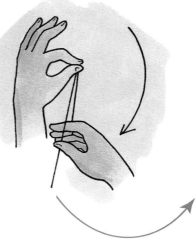

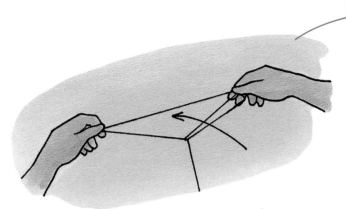

4. Release the string from your free hand. Then reach through the loop and grab another six inches or so of string, pulling the string through the loop to form the "handlebars" of the motorcycle.

Duncan's teams of traveling yo-yo men were just that—all men. It wasn't until the end of the golden days of yo-yo (from 1930 to 1964) that four female demonstrators joined the ranks: Linda ∫engpiel, Loxy Oliver, Donna Walsh, and Helane Zeiger.

5. Touch the spinning yo-yo to the floor and let it "ride" as though you're holding onto the handlebars. Make a roaring sound like that of a motorcycle.

6. To call the yo-yo home, drop the string, give a quick tug, and the yo-yo will return to your hand.

Yo-Yo Tip:
To enhance this trick, either put a metal kazoo in your mouth and use it to generate a loud motorcycle-like sound or make a growling sound like that of a motorcycle.

Walk the Dog and Jump Him Through the Hoop

Who says you can't teach an old dog new tricks?

Yo-Yo Tip:
You might find this trick easier to perform with a "clutch" yo-yo.

1. Start by Walking the Dog.

2. Instead of walking the dog in front of you, bring the yo-yo behind your leg, and walk your yo-yo beneath the leg that is on the same side of your body as your yo-yo hand.

3. Put your yo-yo hand on your hip. Then arch your elbow straight out so that your arm and side form a "hoop."

4. Give the string a slight tug to bring the yo-yo back. If you are using a "clutch" yo-yo, wait for the clutch to engage and return the yo-yo automatically. Let the yo-yo swing around behind you and go "through the hoop."

59

Monkey Climb
the Tree

You don't have to go to a zoo to see this monkey climb a tree. As the yo-yo "climbs" the string, be sure to follow its progress with your eyes.

1. Throw a fast sleeper.

2. Bring your free hand up and slip your forefinger under the middle of the string. With your free hand, lift the spinning yo-yo straight up until it is hanging above your yo-yo hand.

3. Place the string closest to your yo-yo finger inside the groove of the spinning yo-yo. Hold your free hand still and gently pull downward with your yo-yo hand. The yo-yo will appear to "climb" the string.

4. When the yo-yo reaches the top of its climb, slip the string off your finger. The yo-yo will wind up and return to your hand.

In 1962, during the biggest yo-yo craze to that date, 45 million yo-yos were sold in the United States, which at the time had a population of a mere 40 million children.

Thread the Needle

This trick is similar to Monkey Climb the Tree, except that it is performed horizontally. The Monkey climbs the string vertically.

1. Throw a fast sleeper.

2. With your free hand, extend your forefinger, place it under the string, and lift the yo-yo up as if you were going to perform Monkey Climb the Tree.

3. Slip the string through the groove of the spinning yo-yo from behind.

4. Now with your free hand's forefinger between the strings, move your free arm slightly outward and upward. Pull your yo-yo hand backward and "walk" (actually, you will be providing the movement by pulling your yo-yo hand away from the yo-yo) the yo-yo along the string toward your free hand.

Yo-Yo Tip:
Follow the progress of the yo-yo along the string with your eye, as you would do if you were threading a real needle. You might be able to enhance the effect by lifting your arms up near eye level and looking down along the string.

5. As the yo-yo reaches the forefinger of your free hand, slip the finger out of the loop you have just formed, jerk the string, and let the yo-yo wind back up.

The Confederate Flag

Whistle, hum or sing "Dixie" while building this simple string formation trick.

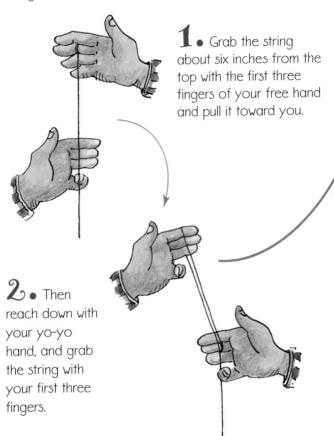

1. Grab the string about six inches from the top with the first three fingers of your free hand and pull it toward you.

2. Then reach down with your yo-yo hand, and grab the string with your first three fingers.

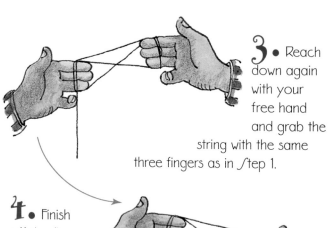

3. Reach down again with your free hand and grab the string with the same three fingers as in Step 1.

4. Finish off the flag by first reaching over with your yo-yo hand's pinky finger, then grabbing the string and pulling it up against your fourth finger. The result should appear as an "X" on its side between two lengths of string. You have just formed a Confederate flag.

Yo-Yo Tip:
Practice this trick with a "dead" (i.e. non-spinning) yo-yo until you've perfected all the moves. Then try it with a fast Sleeper.

Slurp the Spaghetti

You'll love this trick, especially when you ham it up. As you build the trick, make some comments such as "How many of you like spaghetti?" or "Do you know how much fun it is to slurp spaghetti up?"

Yo-Yo Tip:
If you should lose control of the yo-yo, block your teeth with one or both hands so it will strike your hand and not your teeth.

1. Throw a fast sleeper.

2. Reach over with your free hand and grab the yo-yo string about four inches below your yo-yo hand. Hold onto the string with your free hand.

3. Next swing your yo-yo hand down and grab the string about four inches below your free hand. Continue grabbing pieces of string, alternating with fingers of your free and yo-yo hands.

Tom Smothers, the "wacky" member of the Smothers Brothers comedy duo, has been performing his Yo-Yo Man routine since about 1980. It is the hit of the Smothers Brothers' stage shows.

4. Bring the "spaghetti" up to your mouth. Then let go of the string. At the same time make a loud, slurping noise with your mouth. The spinning yo-yo will quickly wind up all the string. It will appear as if you have just sucked the "spaghetti" into your mouth. Pat your stomach, smack your lips, and utter a contented "mmmmm mmmmm," as if you have just enjoyed your meal.

Texas Star

The shining star of Texas is revealed with this string formation trick. This trick is also called Ursa Major.

Yo-Yo Tip:
Practice this trick with a "dead" (i.e. non-spinning) yo-yo. When these moves become automatic, try them after you throw a fast Sleeper.

1. Grab the string with the thumb of your free hand about four to eight inches from the finger-looped end.

2. Swing your yo-yo hand down and catch the string four to eight inches below the thumb of your free hand with your yo-yo hand's ring or pinky finger.

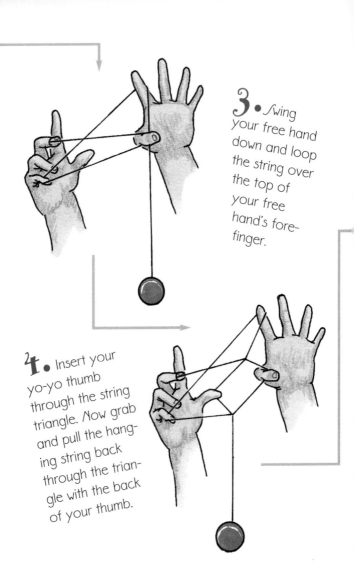

3. Swing your free hand down and loop the string over the top of your free hand's forefinger.

4. Insert your yo-yo thumb through the string triangle. Now grab and pull the hanging string back through the triangle with the back of your thumb.

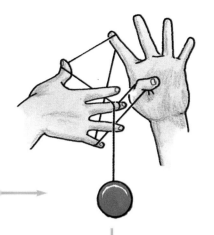

5. Reach down with your yo-yo finger and pull the string a few inches up with the back of the finger.

6. Open up both hands and allow the star-shaped formation to appear between your two hands. Presto! You've made a Texas /tar.

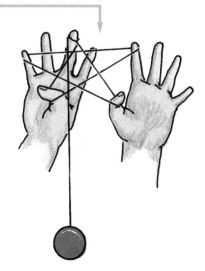

One-Handed Star

Now that you can form a star with two hands, try forming a star with only one hand. This trick is also called Ursa Minor.

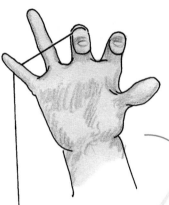

1. Hold your yo-yo hand upright with the string hanging down from the middle finger. Slip your little finger inside the string.

2. Turn your hand slightly and slip your fore-finger under the string.

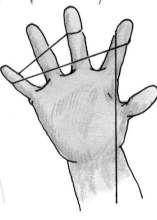

Yo-Yo Tip:
Practice this trick with a "dead" (i.e. non-spinning) yo-yo until you've perfected the trick. Then try the trick with a fast Sleeper.

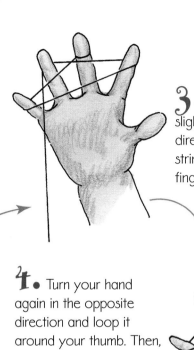

3. Twist your hand slightly in the opposite direction and loop the string around your ring finger.

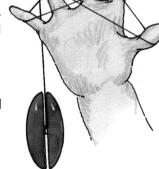

4. Turn your hand again in the opposite direction and loop it around your thumb. Then, twist your hand downward and pick up the string so that it loops around your middle finger, completing the formation of the small star.

5. Open your hand to display the star.

Éiffel Tower

You don't have to spend a lot of money to visit this Eiffel Tower. All you need is your yo-yo!

1. Open your free-hand thumb and forefinger and place it about eight inches below your yo-yo hand and pull the string toward you and up.

2. Bring your yo-yo hand thumb against the string in a counterclockwise motion.

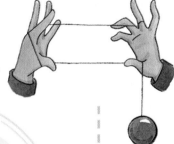

Yo-Yo Tip:
The easiest way to learn this and other "string-formation tricks"—is with a "dead" (i.e. nonspinning) yo-yo. When these moves become automatic, try them after you throw a fast sleeper.

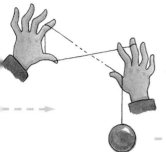

3. Rotate the string clockwise with your free hand to form an "X."

4. Reach over with your free hand and grab the string about 18 inches from the yo-yo, pull it through the triangle, and allow the string to slide off of the outside of your thumb and middle fingers.

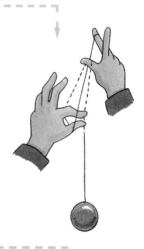

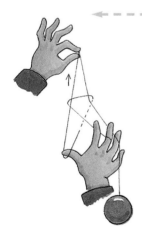

5. Finally, pull the yo-yo string up through the loop you just released while catching the hanging string between the yo-yo and ring finger. Display the Eiffel Tower.

The Man on the Flying Trapeze

Being the daring young man on the flying trapeze will take some practice to perfect. This is generally considered to be the most difficult of all basic yo-yo tricks

Yo-Yo Tip:
Practice, practice, practice! This is a difficult trick to master, but you'll eventually get it. All it takes is a lot of practice and determination. Don't give up after a few tries.

1. Throw a Breakaway, swinging the yo-yo in an upside down arc in front of your body.

2. When the yo-yo starts to rise on the opposite side of your body, extend the index finger of your free hand out so that it strikes the string about three to five inches from the yo-yo. Allow the yo-yo to loop over your outstretched finger.

3. Let the yo-yo swing around your outstretched finger in an arc and land on the string.

4. Now quickly push your hands together, letting the sleeping yo-yo swing back and forth "trapeze" style.

5. To bring it home, quickly pull your hands apart. The yo-yo will fly upward and over your free hand's forefinger, wind up, and return to your yo-yo hand.

Double or Nothing

After you've mastered the Man On The Flying Trapeze, give this trick a try. Surprisingly enough, you may find that this trick is slightly easier.

1. Begin by throwing a Breakaway.

2. When the yo-yo starts to rise on the opposite side of your body, extend the index finger of your free hand on the string about three to five inches from the yo-yo, as if setting up to perform a Man On The Flying Trapeze.

3. Let the yo-yo swing around the out-stretched index finger of your free hand, just as you would for a Man On The Flying Trapeze. Instead, allow the yo-yo to make a bigger circle and swing around your extended index finger of your yo-yo hand.

4. Let it continue swinging around the index finger of your free hand a second time.

5. Catch the yo-yo on one of the strings between your two index fingers, similar to catching the Man On The Flying Trapeze. Push your hands closer together and let the yo-yo hang slightly below your two hands.

6. To exit the trick, pull your hands apart and "pop" the yo-yo into the air. Let all the loose string slip off your fingers and wind up into the yo-yo. Catch the yo-yo with your yo-yo hand.

Pinwheel

The Pinwheel is one of the easiest and most beautiful tricks to perform and watch!

1. Throw a fast *Sleeper*.

2. Grab the string with the thumb and middle finger of the free hand, about two-thirds of the way down.

3. Then move the free hand up and to the side, away from your body, while moving the yo-yo hand down.

4. Swing the hanging yo-yo in circles, performing three or more Pinwheel-like turns.

5. Complete the final turn by throwing the yo-yo forward and up, releasing the string with both hands. Catch the yo-yo in your yo-yo hand, palm up.

Yo-Yo Tip:
If you attempt a Man On The Flying Trapeze and miss catching the yo-yo on the string, you may be able to bluff your audience into thinking you were really performing a Pinwheel!

Warp Drive

Although this trick is difficult to perform, it is an impressive trick to watch when performed smoothly. Another challenging combination trick for the budding yo-yo expert!

> **Yo-Yo Tip:**
> When going from a Loop the Loop into an Around the World, throw the yo-yo slightly outward and farther to the right (for right-handers), away from your body.

1. Begin by throwing a Forward Pass.

2. As the yo-yo returns to your hand, don't catch it. Instead, send it out in front of you as if you were doing Loop the Loop. However, only loop it one time.

3. Go into a second loop, but instead of bringing it straight back toward your hand (as if you were throwing another loop), send it Around the World.

4. Continue alternating a single loop and an Around the World as many times as you can.

Today, the yo-yo appeals equally to boys and girls. In fact, the 1998 World Champion was a girl, 17-year-old Jennifer Baybrook, who beat out all challengers. In the finals, she was the only female.

Bank Deposit

If you're looking for a great trick to end your act, it's time you made a Bank Deposit!

1. Pull your left pants' pocket open as wide as possible.

2. Throw a hard ∫leeper between your legs.

Yo-Yo Tip:
You'll find this trick is easier if your pants' pockets are larger than normal. ∫ome old-time yo-yo experts would have their pants custom-made with large, open pockets to make this trick easier to perform.

3. Let the yo-yo swing around your leg and into your pocket. This will take some practice.

In the mid-1950s, the best-selling yo-yos were made of wood. Yo-yo demonstrators learned the art of "yo-yo carving." With a special woodcutting knife or a regular pocket knife, they would customize each child's yo-yo with beach scenes, birds, and other fun examples of carved figures, plus the child's name.

Rattlesnake

Watch out for the Rattlesnake. It walks and talks like one, but this one doesn't bite! This trick is easier to perform when wearing loose pants.

1. Throw a *Sleeper* with a sideways motion, as if performing a *Sleeping Beauty* (see page 21).

2. Instead of picking up the yo-yo with your free hand, let it spin on its side.

3. Move your leg so that the flailing string brushes against your pants leg. The string should produce a "rattling" sound as it strikes your pants.

Through the Tunnel

Instead of "walking your dog," send your yo-yo through the tunnel. Be careful! This is a tricky trick.

Yo-Yo Tip: This trick is called a Combination Trick, because it combines the elements of several tricks.

1.

Start with your yo-yo hand in a position as if you were going to perform a Throw Down. Instead, throw the yo-yo down and swing it backward, easing into an Around the World backward.

2.
As the yo-yo comes around in front of you, spread your legs approximately two feet apart, and let the yo-yo swing through your legs. Gently land it on the ground behind you.

3.
Perform a Creeper in reverse. Walk the yo-yo along the floor and back to your hand.

Shoot the Moon

Shoot the Moon is an old trick that is similar to Over the Falls (see page 36). However, you direct the yo-yo upward toward the ceiling instead of downward toward the floor.

Yo-Yo Tip:
This can be a dangerous trick. Do not attempt it until you have mastered the basic tricks and have achieved good control over your yo-yo.

1. Begin by throwing a Forward Pass.

2. As the yo-yo returns, flick your wrist in a semicircular motion, sending the yo-yo almost straight up above your head. The yo-yo will pass very close to your face; this is what makes the trick potentially dangerous. Be careful!

3. As the yo-yo comes down, flick your wrist, and send it back out in front of you.

4. As the yo-yo returns, either catch it or, if you prefer, flick it back upward for a second "moon shot."

The first patent application for a yo-yo-like toy was filed at the United States Patent Office in 1866.

The Elephant's Trunk

if you know how to make an elephant sound, add it to this trick!

1. Place a light-weight chair two or three feet in front of you with the back facing you.

Yo-Yo Tip:
You can also perform this trick with an assistant's outstretched arm. Do not attempt to do so unless you have demonstrated full control and have become master of your yo-yo.

2. Throw a fast sleeper.

3. Swing your yo-yo out in front of you and let it come to rest—while still spinning—over the back of the chair. Viola! You've just created an Elephant's Trunk.

4. Give a jerk on the string to bring the yo-yo back to your hand.

Brain Twister

This is truly one of the most impressive tricks to perform. 'Nuff said!

1. Begin by throwing a fast sleeper.

2. Move the forefinger of your free hand forward and under the string. Then lift your free hand up so the yo-yo hangs between your hands.

Yo-Yo Tip:
Go for a single loop when learning this trick. As you become better at the trick, you can add extra loops. This trick is considerably easier to learn if you use a transaxle yo-yo.

3. Now move your yo-yo hand in front of the yo-yo and place the string inside the yo-yo, about 12 inches below your free hand. Halfway between your free hand and the yo-yo, grab the string with the middle finger of your yo-yo hand and pull the string toward you.

4. Bring your free hand forward and down. The yo-yo should flip over the top in a circle.

5. Use your yo-yo hand to bring the yo-yo toward you. Now move the string the other way. This will make the yo-yo go in a reverse direction, up and around, and off the free hand's fore-finger.

6. As the yo-yo unwinds, complete the trick with a clean catch.

Over the years, yo-yos have appeared in other shapes than the classic Imperial and butterfly. Yo-yos have been manufactured and sold in the shape of balls (baseballs, basketballs, golf balls, tennis balls, footballs), globes of the world, truck wheels, flying saucers, and satellites.

Skyrocket

If you want to take a trip into outer space, here's your chance.

1. Start by throwing a fast sleeper.

2. While the yo-yo is sleeping, take the string off the finger of your yo-yo hand with your free hand. Hold the string with your free hand just below the loop.

yo-yo play, especially the more advanced tricks such as The Man on the Flying Trapeze (see page 76), help develop hand-eye coordination.

3. Jerk the string upward and let go of it as the yo-yo passes your hand. The yo-yo will blast off like a sky-rocket. Pull both hands back to clear the way.

4. Once the yo-yo begins to descend, have it "splash down" in your hand. If you want show off a bit, try catching it in your pant's pocket.

Stuart F. Crump, Jr. is known worldwide as "Professor Yo-Yo." He is the author of four yo-yo books, which include *The Bluebook of Yo, It's Yo-Yo Time, The Little Book of Yo-Yos,* and *Let's Yo!* He is also the editor and publisher of the *Yo-Yo Times* newsletter, a quarterly publication for yo-yo enthusiasts. He lives in Herndon, VA, with his wife, four children, dog, two cats, and 500 yo-yos.

For more information on *Yo-Yo Times,* send a self-addressed stamped envelope to: *Yo-Yo Times* newsletter, P.O. Box 1519-PI, Herndon, VA, 20172 or e-mail yoyotime@aol.com.

Cover:
Photography by Jook Leung/FPG International
Illustration by Hank Moorehouse and Anne Kennedy

Illustrators:
Anne Kennedy, Kate Flanagan, John Magine, John Jones, Hank Moorehouse